TURNER

by Jean Selz

CROWN PUBLISHERS, INC. - NEW YORK

Title page: PORTRAIT OF TURNER, BY GEORGE DANCE, 1800
Pencil, 10″ × 7¾″
The Royal Academy, London

Translated by:
EILEEN B. HENNESSEY

Series published under the direction of:
MADELEINE LEDIVELEC-GLOECKNER

PHOTOGRAPHY BY: BRIDGEMAN-COOPER LIBRARY, London - JOHN WEBB, London - A. J. WYATT, Philadelphia.

NORTH-WEST VIEW, 1787   Watercolor, 12⅛" × 17"   British Museum, London

ENGLAND AND THE LANDSCAPE

The work of Joseph Mallord William Turner represents a unique phenomenon in the history of painting: the successive achievement of two diametrically opposed styles of expression, implying a radical transformation of the sense of perception, the first style based on the continuation of an esthetic past, the second providing an example of a vision whose revolutionary power would be revealed in time to come

The fact that this transition between two worlds of artistic creation, which marks the break between the classical age and modern times, was accomplished during the first half of the nineteenth century is not the least remarkable aspect of this phenomenon.

EDINBURGH, 1801   Watercolor, 7¾″ × 5″   British Museum, London

The Mer de Glace, Chamonix, 1802   Pencil, watercolor and wash, $12^3/_8'' \times 18^7/_{16}''$ British Museum, London

It is also a disturbing factor, when we consider that strictly speaking it is not a logical evolution in Turner's work: his first style of painting cannot in any way be regarded as the first experimental, tentative stage in his future development.

In the various periods that may reveal a new orientation in a painter's work, we note the achievement of a greater maturity in the technique of his draughtsmanship or in the use of color, or, as in the cases of Van Gogh and Bonnard, a discovery of light, manifested in a change of palette. But the same eye and the same hand are recognizable in both styles. Van Gogh's very somber early style of painting in Holland was not at all academic or classical; his broad, agitated brushstrokes were already indicative of a tormented state of mind. In his transition from Fauvism to pure abstraction, Kandinsky retained the same colors and a similar lyrical mode of expression; despite an equally radical change, his two styles could not have warranted a statement that they belonged to two different painters. This is not true of Turner.

Another strange fact in this pictorial revolution, which opens a new chapter in the history of art, is that it occurred in England. Enduring traditions have never deprived the English of being daring individuals. But in painting, before Turner and long after, we find in England none of those movements that revolutionized the conceptions of artistic creation in France, Germany, Scandinavia, and prerevolutionary Russia. There is no English name of importance in the Impressionist, Expressionist, Fauvist, or Cubist movements. (Sisley was a British subject, but he was born in Paris and spent almost all of his life in France.) The only notable movement to appear in England in the nineteenth century was Pre-Raphaelitism, which represented an attempt to return to the esthetics of a distant past.

This singularity, however, is not completely inexplicable. In order to understand it, we must first note that the history of English painting differs considerably from that of French painting. Surprisingly, the French painters turned only belatedly to the landscape. In this connection it is noteworthy that literature and even philosophy had very little influence on painting. In the 1770s and 1780s painters were preoccupied not with a « return to nature » but with a return to Antiquity. In the studios, models were dressed up as Greeks and Romans and made to enact historical scenes in settings in which skillfully reconstructed architectural structures were much more important than trees, flowers, and streams. This was at a time when Jean-Jacques Rousseau had already written his last book, *Les Rêveries du promeneur solitaire,* in which he turns away from human beings in order to contemplate nature (« The moment I stand under the trees in the midst of the foliage, I think I am in paradise on earth, and I enjoy an inner pleasure as keen as if I were the happiest of mortal beings »).

However, a certain realism in landscape, not without its conventions, had already been practiced by the Dutch painters of the seventeenth century, and the Italian *vedute* (« views ») painters of the eighteenth century had set themselves the task of painting extremely detailed views of cities. This, however, had not won them official approval; it was not until 1763, five years before his death, that Canaletto was admitted to the Academy of Venice. But he was highly esteemed in London (where he had gone at the behest of Joseph Smith, the British consul at Venice and a patron of the arts) and where he lived for several years.

THE AMATEUR ARTIST, 1802–1810 Pen and brown ink and wash with some
watercolor and scraping out, 7¼″ × 11⅞″ British Museum, London

XXVIII

Old London Bridge, 1796   Pencil, 10⅝″ × 7¾″   British Museum, London

Distant View of Rochester, 1793   Pencil, 8¼" × 10¾"   British Museum, London

The fact that Paul Sandby (1725–1809) owned a collection of Canaletto's paintings is interesting, because Sandby was the inaugurator of landscape painting in England. This is not to say that the English painters' new predilection for landscape came directly from Italy. The fact is that its sources traveled by way of Switzerland, and slightly later it was the mountainous sites of the Alpine chain that gave the landscapists their romantic character. Sandby himself never left England, where he was the first to use watercolor as an independent medium of expression and the first to practice the technique of aquatint. But the landscape enjoyed its great burst of creativity, in a coherent union of realistic observation and romantic imagination, with John Robert Cozens (1752–1797). He was familiar with Switzerland and Italy, and could have been Turner's companion there, had he not died insane at the age of forty-five. We shall consider Cozens's relationship to Turner's work later in this book.

Another important name among the English landscapists of the end of the eighteenth century is that of Thomas Girtin (1775–1802), another great watercolorist whose personality is evident in a certain freedom in his use of color. Previously watercolor had always been regarded by artists as a means of coloring drawings («tinted drawings,» the English called them) rather than as a technique of painting. We shall see that this kind of autonomy of color — barely glimpsed by Girtin — would later constitute Turner's fundamental innovation.

THE ENTHUSIAST OF CATHEDRALS

Turner was born on April 23, 1775, in London's Maiden Lane, near Covent Garden Market, into an England that was sensitive both to the charm of its countryside and to the way in which painters depicted it. It was undoubtedly difficult to ascertain the date of his birth, for in a lecture given in 1853, two years after the painter's death, his friend and early admirer John Ruskin (to whom we shall refer later) was unable to say exactly how old Turner was at his death because his birth records had been destroyed in a fire.

Turner's father, a native of Devonshire, was a barber. Although he would have preferred to see his son adopt the same trade, he was exceptionally understanding and never raised any opposition to the boy's early demonstration of his fondness for drawing. In fact, he encouraged the child's gifts, and William was fervently devoted to his father throughout his life. But his childhood years were not without their difficult periods, caused by his mother, whose passionate nature and rages ultimately led to her insanity. In 1800 she had to be hospitalized in Bethlehem Hospital (now the Imperial War Museum), and she died insane in an asylum in 1804.

What caused the awakening, in this young city boy, of that fondness for nature

SELF-PORTRAIT, c. 1798   Oil, 29¼″ × 23″   Tate Gallery, London

PLOUGHING UP TURNIPS, NEAR SLOUGH (WINDSOR), 1805–1811
Oil, 40⅛″ × 51¼″   Tate Gallery, London

14

THE FALL OF AN AVALANCHE IN THE GRISONS, 1810
Oil, 35½″ × 67¼″   Tate Gallery, London

Walton Reach, c. 1807 Panel, 14½″ × 29″ Tate Gallery, London

which was gradually to make him the greatest landscapist of his time? He apparently did not become acquainted with the countryside until the age of ten, when he spent some time at the home of his maternal uncle, J. M. W. Marshall, a butcher in Brentford. His first extant drawings date from 1787, when he was twelve. They are copies of prints by various artists, like the engraving *North-West View*, published in Oxford in 1780 and the subject of Turner's first watercolor. These early attempts, though conscientious, are awkward, but thanks to the constant practice of drawing he made rapid progress, even earning a few shillings a drawing from purchasers.

His first sketchbook still in existence, the *Oxford Sketch Book*, is a small, oblong album six by ten inches, with garishly colored covers. Done around 1789, it already showed landscape studies: a church, houses, trees, and cows drawn in black lead or ink, and one watercolor drawing showing a young man holding his horse by the bridle.

Turner's first commissions were for illustrations for small popular books, guides, and calendars. He was soon drawing boats on the Thames, and in London and its environs and at Margate he discovered the sea. But in this early period Turner was particularly interested in old homes, castles, Gothic churches, and ruins. His drawings of these subjects appeared in various publications. In his early paintings we see some hints of the importance later to be assumed by architectural structures as a romantic theme.

His early teachers included Palice, a painter of flowers in Soho, the architect Thomas Hardwick, and Thomas Malton, whose style of depicting monuments was copied by Turner. In December 1789, at the age of fourteen, Turner enrolled in the Royal Academy schools, where in the following year his watercolor *The Archbishop's Palace, Lambeth* was exhibited. Ten years later he was admitted to the Royal Academy as an associate.

In a sketchbook of 1791 (*Bristol and Malmesbury Sketch Book*), his meticulous concern for the complicated perspectives of these cathedrals and abbeys, drawn with the tip of a finely pointed pencil, is already evident. The sketchbook also contains watercolor landscapes, the park of a castle, a stream in a valley, and the ruins of a church. Their coloring is still rather heavy, but all of them are harmoniously arranged on the page, with a feeling for space which was always one of Turner's notable qualities. In 1793 he received a prize from the Society of Arts for a landscape drawing.

At this time he had already begun his wanderings about the English countryside and his tours of cities, which throughout his life were to supply him with subjects for the major part of his work. Through his drawings we are able to follow the itinerary of his movements year by year. In 1793 he was in the southeast, at Rochester, Canterbury, and Dover. A pencil *View of Rochester*, with the city in the background seen through some boats in the middle ground and trees in the foreground, served as a model for a watercolor reproduced as an engraving (the first engraving made from a work by Turner) in the *Cooper Plate Magazine* for May 1, 1794.

In 1794 Turner explored the Midlands. He spent the next two years traveling in southern Wales and Sussex, where he stayed in Brighton. In 1797 he was in the Lake District in the north. These travels are reminiscent of the wanderings of Corot, paintbox in hand, about France. Both artists had to sacrifice to this activity the stability of their existence; their passion for work and their constant search for the landscape to be

Storm off Dover, 1793   Watercolor (unfinished), 10″ × 14¼″   British Museum, London

discovered denied both of them any hope of a home life. During this period Turner exhibited regularly at the Royal Academy: five watercolors in 1795, ten in 1796.

His favorite landscape was always a bit of countryside with a river gently threading through it. But what he loved above all to draw was cathedrals (preferably Gothic) and old castles. Ruskin was later to reproach him for having wasted his youth painting «completely uninteresting subjects — parks, villas, and in general ugly architectural structures.» However, Turner's diligence in drawing monuments, some of which were extremely complicated structures, helped him to acquire the knowledge that enabled him to become a teacher of perspective. He was not very good at drawing human beings; there are very few in his sketches, and they never played a major role in his landscapes.

Using a fine-tipped black lead pencil and sheets of paper ranging in size from

Brigantine, 1802   Pencil, 4³/₈" × 7¹/₄"   From « Small Calais Pier » Sketchbook

fourteen by eighteen inches (he seldom used anything larger) down to three by five inches, or more generally countless sketchbooks, he drew extremely detailed studies or quick, unworked sketches. It was not his intention that the drawing in these «scribblings» should be regarded as an independent medium of expression in its own right. Nevertheless he was careful to keep his sketchbooks, some of which are quaintly bound in leather and have four metal clasps, which gives them a faintly medieval appearance.

In the sketchbooks we frequently find a stylistic technique which Turner was not the only artist to use, and which consists in marking a line with dots pressed into the paper, as if to more securely fix the structure of the monument being drawn. This type of «punctuation» is found later in the drawings of Ingres (who certainly had not seen Turner's work), particularly in his landscape drawings done in Rome after his move to the Villa Medici in 1806. In contrast, it is not impossible that Corot, who used the same procedure in his works, particularly his drawings of the Roman countryside, may have seen the drawings of Ingres done twenty years earlier. But perhaps this is a practice quickly acquired by anyone who has ever held a sharpened pencil.

In any event both Turner and Thomas Girtin followed this practice for a time (the dotted lines are very visible through the color in the latter's watercolors), and it is difficult to say who influenced whom. Turner and Girtin were the same age, and they worked together at the Monro School starting in 1794 or 1795. This school, established by Dr. Thomas Monro, was to play a major role in the history of watercolor in England. Its evening courses were attended by young artists, who were set to work copying the paintings of the best watercolorists, particularly those of John Robert Cozens. Judging

Fishing Boats with distant Castle on Rock (probably Harlech Castle), 1798
Monochrome wash, 9¾" × 12½"   British Museum, London

Dido Building Carthage, 1815
Oil, 61¼″ × 91¼″   National Gallery, London

THE BAY OF BAIÆ WITH APOLLO AND THE SIBYL, c. 1823 Oil, 57¼″ × 94″   Tate Gallery, London

GEORGE IV AT A BANQUET IN EDINBURGH, 1822
Oil, 27″ × 36⅛″   Tate Gallery, London

24

by the results obtained, this method was excellent, because among those who attended Dr. Monro's establishment we find the names of John Sell Cotman, John Varley, and Peter De Wint, in addition to Turner and Girtin. Turner worked here for three years, and he undoubtedly owed to the study of Cozens's landscapes much of the attraction he felt for the romantic sites that characterize his early painting. Unquestionably he also perfected his practice of watercolor here, for after 1798 a definite evolution can be seen in his work.

THE LESSON OF CLAUDE LORRAIN

In 1795 Turner was twenty years old. Until then he had done nothing but drawing and watercolor, to which he devoted himself with unflagging application. Now, however, he became interested in oil painting, and in 1796 for the first time he exhibited at the Royal Academy a painting called *Fishermen at Sea* (F. W. A. Fairfax-Cholmeley Collection, on permanent loan to the Tate Gallery). It is a moonlight view of Needles Point, the strange rocks in Alum Bay on the Isle of Wight. This site, where Turner had stayed during the preceding year, is famous for its varicolored sand cliffs.

From this time on praise was no stranger to Turner. In 1797 Anthony Pasquin wrote of him that, « He seems to have a special vision of nature, and the exceptional character of his perceptions includes a skill such that this artist succeeds in rendering the transparency and the movements of the sea with a perfection not generally seen in paintings. »

This somewhat belated achievement of a new medium of expression was to quickly produce in Turner's mind a new conception of the work to be painted. In his first canvases, those exhibited in 1798 and 1799 at the Royal Academy, Turner is still visibly devoted to the favored subjects — romantic lakes and castles — that dominated in his watercolors, and which had won for him numerous commissions. Now, however, he turned to compositions in which the landscape acted as a setting for some scene inspired by the literature of Antiquity. An example is the painting *Aeneas and the Sibyl*, painted around 1800, which belongs to the tradition of the « historical landscape, » a genre greatly esteemed at the end of the eighteenth century despite the success of the watercolorists, whose naturalistic tendency had already caused an evolution in people's visions.

The choice of such subjects was not irrelevant to Turner's ambition to become a member of the Royal Academy (as previously mentioned, he became an associate member in 1799 and attained full membership in 1802). His *Self-Portrait* in the Tate Gallery dates from this period. It shows a blond man with a sensual mouth and eyes both alert and dreamy, wearing an elegant cravat knotted in the fashion of the dandies of his day. He was already sought out as a painter, and commissions were numerous. His life became

VIEW OF A CITY, c. 1830
Watercolor, 9¾″ × 12″   British Museum, London

VENICE: THE CAMPANILE OF ST. MARK'S AND THE DOGE'S PALACE, 1819
Watercolor, 8¾″ × 11⅜″   British Museum, London

27

more independent, and a hint of passion appeared: he left his fathers's barbershop in Maiden Lane and went to live in Harley Street with the widowed actress Sarah Danby and her four children, who became five with the birth of Turner's daughter Evelina. This liaison apparently did not survive after 1810.

In the large compositions to which he devoted himself in the early years of the nineteenth century, he alternated between biblical subjects and seascapes. In 1800 he painted *The Fifth Plague of Egypt* (Art Association of Indianopolis), which William Beckford, the author of *Vathek,* purchased from him. In 1801 appeared *Fishing Boats in the Gale* (London, National Gallery), in 1802 *The Tenth Plague of Egypt* (Tate Gallery). These paintings, however, did not cause him to abandon his watercolor work.

From a trip to Scotland in 1801 he brought back numerous drawings and watercolors in which the influence exerted on his work by the practice of oil painting can be discerned. The very nature of the Scottish landscapes to which he applied himself, and whose lakes and castles of course inspired him, prompted him to use color in simplified masses, which is a very remote but fortuitous augury of the future orientation of Turner's esthetics. This can be seen, for example, in the watercolor entitled *Edinburgh, View of St. Margaret's Lake with Mount Calton at Right* (British Museum). The color, applied in patches with vague shapes, is almost monochromatic, being limited to gray tones that are both warm and delicate. A few clouds tint the paper, left white for the sky. In *Inverary,* the monochromy of a lake surrounded by mountains reveals, in sufficiently striking manner to warrant mention, that yellow tonality of which the painter was to become so fond many years later. This color came to be designated «Turner yellow» in the analytical list of his palette. But these few indications, which can be considered premonitory signs, were certainly not perceived as such by Turner himself, and they were to remain in eclipse for a long time before bearing their fruit.

Until now the Napoleonic wars had prevented Turner from crossing the frontiers of the Continent. But four months after the signing of the Treaty of Peace in Amiens on March 25, 1802, he disembarked at Calais, under exciting conditions which his pencil captured in some forty drawings in the *Calais Pier Sketch Book.* The following year this supplied him with the subject for a painting, *The Calais Pier* (Tate Gallery), which is full of the beautiful movement of an agitated sea, dancing sails, and frightened people. But the paint is handled rather dryly, and the *Times* critic spoke of the work in somewhat unpleasant terms: «It offers a lamentable example of genius lost in affectation and degenerating into absurdity. Under the pretext of obtaining overall effects, in most cases the artist obtains only effects of confusion and incongruity. His sea resembles soap, chalk, smoke, and a thousand other things. The sky overhanging it is nothing more than a heaping up of marble mountains not a all in harmony with the sea.»

Turner spent some time in Paris, and of course paid long visits to the Louvre, where Napoleon had installed his booty of art works brought back from Italy. He paid particular attention to Correggio, Domenichino, Giorgione, Poussin, Rubens, and Ruysdael, and made numerous sketches and even watercolor copies of Titian. His Louvre *Sketch Book* also contains many notes about these painters, and an analysis of the colors used by Rembrandt, which was visibly of use to him later for certain paintings. Concerning *Tobias and the Angel* he wrote, «Is rich in colour and brilliant in effect but hard.»

SUNSET ON THE GRAND CANAL OF VENICE, 1825   Watercolor, 4½″ × 7⁷/₁₆″   British Museum, London

Life Study -
Female Figure, 1798
Colored chalks and
watercolor
8½" × 5½"
British Museum
London

*Academy Study -
Standing Male Figure
1800–1805
Pen and ink with
bistre and
white chalk
7⅛" × 10¾"
British Museum
London*

31

RIVER WITH TREES: SUNSET, 1820–1830
Watercolor, 12⅛″ × 19⅜″ British Museum, London

A Castle on a Headland, c. 1824
Watercolor, 10¹⁄₈″ × 10⁵⁄₈″ British Museum, London

Kilchurn Castle on Loch Awe, 1801   Black and white chalk finished in pencil, 14¼″ × 18¾″   British Museum, London

In Europe he was attracted to the regions which had made the romantic painters successful in England: Savoy, Piedmont, Saint Gothard, Mont Blanc, the Rhine falls at Schaffhausen, and the Swiss lakes in their magnificent settings. From his travels in these regions he brought back an abundant harvest of drawings. We now begin to see the parallel double track followed by Turner in his works: on the one hand he studied nature enthusiastically in pencil and watercolor, on the other he continued a pictorial activity in which nature, notwithstanding the role he assigned to it, acts only as an imaginary setting for scenes inspired by literature, mythology, and the Bible. *The Holy Family, Venus and Adonis, Echo and Narcissus, The Destruction of Sodom, The Goddess*

A Scotch Loch,   1801   Pencil   British Museum, London

of Discord Choosing the Apple of Contention in the Garden of the Hesperides — these
are the themes in which classicism and romanticism are blended, sometimes quite skillfully «He could become another Claude Lorrain,» wrote the *Morning Post.* But nothing
in these very sophisticated compositions hints at the future Turner.

It is evident that Poussin for the allegorical landscape, Claude Lorrain for landscape *per se,* and Van de Velde for seascapes were the principal masters to whose level
Turner's art sought to rise. Claude's influence was the strongest. However, his instruction
was not as pernicious as claimed by Ruskin, who showed a great deal of irritation.
«Turner never recovered from it,» he wrote in his *Modern Painters.* «His compositions

THE HARBOR OF DIEPPE, c. 1826
Oil, 68⅜″ × 88¾″   The Frick Collection, New York

36

My Landing at Calais
1800–1805
Black and white
chalk, 17½" × 10¾"
From
« Calais Pier »
Sketchbook

NYMPHEUM OF ALESSANDRO SEVERO, 1819
Watercolor, 14½″ × 8¼″   British Museum, London

ARCHWAY WITH TREES BY THE SEA, 1828
Oil, 23⅝″ × 34½″   Tate Gallery, London

A House among Trees, 1799–1802   Monochrome wash, 16¼″ × 10½″
British Museum, London

were always mannered, cold, and sometimes even silly.» Ruskin's severity, be it noted in passing, would not prevent him from being the fervent defender of the painter's later and most contested style.

Claude Lorrain and his *Liber Veritatis*, a series of 195 drawings, served as the inspiration for Turner's *Liber Studiorum*, comprising 71 compositions begun in 1806 and worked on until around 1810. Claude had made these pen drawings, painted with bistre or India ink wash, an index of his principal paintings. Turner utilized the same technique, sometimes awkwardly and even clumsily in the case of depiction of the human figures. However, it is in the plates of the *Liber Studiorum* that we find his best realized drawings. These are not outlines, studies, or quick sketches, but compositions intended for engraving. (They were in fact sometimes engraved by Turner himself. The mezzotint edition was copied in a very linear series of etchings.) We find here all of Turner's favorite subjects, summarized in the subtitle on the frontispiece indicating the various types of landscapes: «Historical, mountainous, pastoral, marine, and architectural.»

There is thus no thematic unity to the work. The only link between the plates is

40

Mortlake Terrace, the Seat of William Moffat, Summer's Evening, 1827
Oil, 36¼″ × 48⅛″   National Gallery of Art, Washington D.C. (Andrew Mellon Collection)

CHICHESTER CANAL, c. 1830–1831
Oil, 25¾″ × 53″   Tate Gallery, London

the author's graphic style. Reminiscences of Antiquity and biblical scenes stand side by side with views of the Alps and the glacier, London seen from Greenwich, and, of course, English streams and castles, old mills and cathedrals. One of the most beautiful wash drawings in the *Liber Studiorum,* and the most typical of Turner's vision, is *The Junction of Severn and Wye*, in which the two rivers form part of a landscape with infinite depths. In his English landscapes and his seascapes, the painter frequently made use of this plunging of the eye into distances that are both present and vague.

During his years of work on this collection, Turner continued his wanderings about the country, the inexhaustible source of his inspiration. In his sketchbooks dating from between 1806 and 1810, we find more than five hundred drawings, not counting perspective studies. He also did a complete series of paintings, including views of Windsor, *The Thames near Walton Bridge,* and other landscapes painted from nature, something he rarely did. He also undertook large compositions after long studio preparation; these included *The Battle of Trafalgar,* and genre scenes such as *A Country Farrier Discussing the Price of the Shoe* (an abridgment of the actual title, which is much longer, although not the longest of the titles Turner often enjoyed inventing). The exhibition of this work in 1807 at the Royal Academy did not prevent him from also showing his works in the private gallery he had opened to the public in 1804/1805 in his home on Harley Street.

In 1807 Turner became a teacher of perspective at the Royal Academy. At this time, and during the following decade, he was esteemed for a style still conditioned by the romantic charm of Claude Lorrain: beautiful effects of aerial perspective, settings for historical themes, majestic trees, and complicated structures. He did not greatly deviate from this formula, except in a few watercolors and in canvases inspired by Philippe-Jacques de Loutherbourg (1740–1812), in which he used the notes from his tour of the Grisons, as in the *Cottage Destroyed by an Avalanche* (1810).

The large paintings on which he now established his prestige, *Dido Building Carthage* (1815) and *The Decline of the Carthaginian Empire* (1817), are ambitious, quite theatrical works full of qualities for a public educated by classical painting. They are not marked by any genuine originality. However, Turner considered *Dido Building Carthage* one of his best works, and he expressed the wish that it should one day be exhibited, together with *Sun Rising Through Vapour* (1807), next to Claude Lorrain's works. He felt that such a juxtaposition would be warranted.

The paintings from this period are certainly not lacking in a certain poetic grace when a beautiful landscape serves as their setting, as in *Apullia in Search of Appullus* (1814), or when the landscape itself is more important than the scenes depicted, as in *Crossing the Brook* (1815). In any event they had their enthusiasts, and they were beginning to command a good price among collectors.

Lord Egremont was one of the painter's most ardent admirers. He began purchasing Turner's paintings in 1810, and several years later Turner became a frequent guest at his home at Petworth in Sussex. He also stayed more than once with Mr. Walter Fawkes at Farnley Hall in Yorkshire, and with Sir John Leicester at Tabley House in Cheshire. When Fawkes, who had become a close friend of Turner, exhibited his collection at his home, Turner submitted some sixty watercolors, and eight of his paintings appeared in the collection of Sir John Leicester, exhibited in 1819.

◁ COLOGNE: THE ARRIVAL OF A PACKET BOAT, 1826   45
  Oil, 66⅜″ × 88¼″   The Frick Collection, New York

THE RED BRIDGE, c. 1830
Watercolor, 12″ × 15″   British Museum, London

FIGURES IN A STORM, c. 1830
Watercolor, 14¼″ × 20⅝″   British Museum, London

Turner returned to the Continent in 1817. He wanted to see Waterloo, and, attracted by the old castles, he spent some time on the banks of the Rhine. In 1819 Italy beckoned, and he went to Venice by way of Mont Cenis, with stops in Turin, Lake Como, and Milan.

The influence of his discovery of Venice on Turner's work can be compared to the influence of Van Gogh's discovery of Provence. While the influence of the southern light upon the Dutch painter was immediate, Turner imparted the effects of his overwhelming Venetian experience to his painting only with a certain deliberate slowness. Nevertheless, a new quality evident in such watercolors as *La Salute, The Campanile, and the Ducal Palace Seen from the Canal*, and *The Nympheum of Alessandro Severo* heralds the extraordinary mastery of color to be revealed in his watercolors.

Perhaps Rome, his next place of work, had *a priori* a greater attraction for him, and it may have been the true goal of his tour. He was hoping to find in its buildings and museums that atmosphere of ancient and classical grandeur useful for the kind of paintings that had won such great success for him and which he planned to continue painting. This is what he did in canvases like *Rome Seen from the Vatican*, painted in 1820 after his return to London by way of Naples and a year-end sojourn in Florence.

This painting gives evidence of laborious work. Turner, still concerned with a subject that «tells a story,» and still preoccupied with describing beautiful architectural perspectives, shows Raphael and La Fornarina on the balcony of the pontifical palace overlooking the city. An incorrect symmetry imparts to it a strange awkwardness, and one would say that Turner had lost some of his liking for such compositions. This impression is still more striking when we compare the painting with the drawing, done on gray paper with pen and brown ink and touches of white gouache, which he had done in Rome the previous year, and which has the same title and the same view without the invented balcony scene (Turner Bequest, No. CLXXXIX-41). The drawing is much more beautiful than the painting, its composition is more harmonious, its perspective truer. The studio work seems to have disoriented Turner in his transposition of the drawing to the painting. Venice disturbed something in him, but the time had not yet come for this disturbance to be manifested in a completely new method of expression.

Undoubtedly a certain prudence also warned him not to risk losing his clientele, especially since in 1821 he was having a new gallery built in his home on Queen Ann Street, Turner was not a man to undertake such an expenditure lightly. He was always very attentive to financial questions, and he left behind him a harsh reputation for avarice and even stinginess — although, according to Ruskin, this did not prevent him from having moments of generosity.

In 1822 he had to absorb some more of England, and he made a trip to Scotland. One painting — *George IV at a Banquet, in Edinburgh* — contains a special memory of the trip, but he does not seem to have been very satisfied with it. Here again, in the exaggerated perspective of the long table which seems to extend into infinity, and in the

Two Women and a Letter, c. 1835   Oil, 148″ × 36″   Tate Gallery, London

LANDSCAPE, c. 1830
Oil, 37⅝″ × 49¼″   Musée de Louvre, Paris

KEELMEN HEAVING IN COALS BY NIGHT, 1835
Oil, 36¼″ × 48¼″   National Gallery of Art, Washington D.C. (Widener Collection)

colors, in which the gold tones and vermilions of the clothing are eroded by the light from the great crystal chandeliers, we feel that something other than the subject itself disturbed Turner. Was he perhaps beginning to discover that color needs freedom?

This question found an answer in another canvas, painted the following year, *The Bay of Baiæ with Apollo and the Sibyl* of 1823. The subject was in accordance with the painter's current line, but it is treated with an ease that harmonizes with the composition of the picture, in which Apollo and the Sibyl stand under the shade of two beautiful trees, while in the hazy distance blue mountains slope down to the sea. The drawing of

Dutch Boats in a Gale, 1800–1805
Pen and ink, wash and white chalk, 17⅛" × 10¾"   British Museum, London

Durham Castle Cathedral, 1799–1802   Pencil, 16¼″ × 10½″   British Museum, London

the landscape is not detailed; it is modeled by light colored masses. The details to which Turner had previously devoted himself are completely absent from this painting. He has now set off on the road of a poetic conception of color which was to reach fruition several years later.

We also find certain indications of this in several watercolors of the same period, while in others the future Turner still seems far in the future. But we already understand what Ruskin meant in *Modern Painters*, in connection with the «Turner topography,» when he contrasted poetic art with historical art: «The art of relating facts faithfully, and the art of relating them with imagination.» Actually this is not only an imagination of facts but also an imagination of the properly pictorial form.

In 1825 Turner again left England for a visit to Holland, Belgium, and Germany. As always he brought back numerous sketches, particularly of the Meuse, the Moselle, and the Rhine, the subjects of which reappeared the following year in his watercolors. But this trip was only a prelude to and a detour from a renewal of his Venetian experience. The Italian light had not yet revealed to him the secret of its charm. In the meantime, he

Durham Castle and Bridge, 1800–1802   Pencil, 10¼″ × 16¼″   British Museum, London

completed some commissions for the architect John Nash, and drew a series of views of *Rivers of England,* intended for engraving.

In 1828 he went to Rome for the second time. If we follow his itinerary through the drawings contained in his albums, he crossed France by way of Orléans, Lyon, and Marseilles, then went on to Italy via Genoa, going first to Florence and Orvieto. But the chronology of his sketchbooks cannot always be deciphered. We know that his return voyage, in January 1829, was a repetition of his first trip, by stagecoach, through the Mont Cenis pass, and that both trips were rather lively adventures.

The painting entitled *Orvieto* shows that Turner's esthetic ideas had not yet changed, but it is a painting without any literary theme. It shows a fountain surrounded by washerwomen, a single tree, a long valley, an old bridge, and the immense expanse into the depths of a delicately colored landscape.

The following year (1829), in contrast, he turned to legend for a subject, *Ulysses Deriding Polyphemus.* Despite the conventional theme, however, this is a work in which the light from an extravagant sun seems to cause the explosion of the entire composition

55

with its ancient sailboats and wild crags — a canvas which Turner could not have painted before his return to Italy. A very old sketch served as the basis for the picture, but because of an irrational lighting the color and the movement of the shadows and lights constitute the splendor of the painting and impart a fantastic quality to it. «Until the time of Claude,» Ruskin wrote, «no one had thought of painting the sun.» (This statement can, however, be challenged. We need only remember the strange sun painted by Altdorfer in his *Battle of Alexander* in the sixteenth century.) But Claude's suns, unlike this one, never had such power of eruption. That palette of golden shades which was to become so dear to the painter, and which without Italy undoubtedly would never have become his preferred palette, had finally exploded.

It is not surprising that the painting was not kindly treated by the critics. The Morning Herald said, «Here is a canvas in which truth, nature, and feeling are sacrificed

Peat Bog, Scotland, 1809   Drawing from «Liber Studiorum»

VALLEY OF AOSTA - SNOWSTORM, AVALANCHE AND THUNDERSTORM, 1836–1837
Oil, 36″ × 48¼″   The Art Institute, Chicago (The Frederick T. Haskell Collection)

THE BURNING OF THE HOUSE OF LORDS AND COMMONS, 16TH OF OCTOBER, 1834
Oil, 36¼″ × 48½″   Philadelphia Museum of Art (John H. McFadden Collection)

58

THE BURNING OF THE HOUSES OF PARLIAMENT, 1834–1835
Oil, 36½″ × 48½″   Cleveland Museum of Art (John L. Severance Collection)

THE SLAVE SHIP, c. 1840   Oil, 35¾″ × 48″
Museum of Fine Arts, Boston (Henry Lillie Pierce Fund)

Scene on French Coast, 1806–1810
Print of etching of above subjeet washed with sepia, 7¹/₁₆″ × 10¹/₁₆″   From «Liber Studiorum»

to melodramatic effect ... *Ulysses Deriding Polyphemus* can be regarded as an example of color in delirium.» In this connection it is interesting to note how hostile the critics were to color until the beginning of the twentieth century. Their blindness before Turner's paintings, which was to be still more dismaying in his last period, reappeared in the time of the Impressionists and the Fauves. But long before, as early as the sixteenth century, Vasari had reproached Paolo Uccello for painting «the fields blue, the cities red, and the various buildings according to his whim.»

In 1829 Turner returned to France. He spent some time in Paris, and traveled through various provinces, including Brittany, Normandy, the Orléanais, Anjou, and Touraine. His watercolors include views of numerous rivers and several French châteaux.

The same year was marked, sadly, by the death of the old barber, his father. In the solitude in which he was forced to spend the greater part of his life, Turner had

Junction of Severn and Wye, 1806–1810   Brown wash, 7³/₁₆″ × 10³/₈″   From « Liber Studiorum »

found a genuine friend in this father, and to the end he surrounded him with an affectionate and unflagging solicitude.

I do not know whether we should postulate a relationship between this death and the change of esthetics, which timid experiments had barely hinted at, and which asserted itself in Turner's painting with striking visibility after 1830. It is not absurd to think that respect for the father may be linked with a respect for tradition, and that unbeknownst to the painter this respect undoubtedly prevented him from breaking resolutely with his customary manner of expressing himself. Now he was suddenly free of all filial bonds, and this liberty may have found its natural expansion in a spiritual independence favorable to a realization of his true personality. In any event, Turner now entered upon the most important period of his work.

Castle of Aosta, 1802   Charcoal drawing with some white gouache, $11^3/_{16}" \times 8^1/_2"$ British Museum, London

«COLOUR BEGINNINGS»

In the inventory of Turner's works prepared, with some difficulty, by A. J. Finberg, the artist's principal biographer, the watercolors and drawings are classified according to an approximate chronology. No other system could be possible with an artist who was careless about dating. In this catalogue, titles — names of countries and cities — grouping several sketchbooks of drawings, and boxes and cartons of watercolors, make a geographical examination of this immense body of work possible, but leave some doubt about the years in which certain trips were made. This is true, for example, of the

Stonehenge, c. 1810   Drawing prepared for «Liber Studiorum»

painter's second voyage to Venice; there is nothing to permit a definite affirmation that it took place in 1832, 1833, or 1835.

Sometimes the designation is as brief as «Colour Studies» or, even more vaguely, «Miscellaneous.» The title «Colour Beginnings» appears at number LXIII; it covers 390 watercolors painted between 1820 and 1830. In this decade the last items are the ones probably best described by this title. Keeping in mind the fact that Turner was fifty-five years old in 1830, what does this sudden announcement of «colour beginnings» mean for his development?

CCXLIV 8 8

Martello Towers near Bexhill, Sussex, 1806–1810   Drawing, 7¼" × 10¾"   From « Liber Studiorum »

It cannot be said that during his romantico-classical period Turner was not a colorist. By this we mean that he was sufficiently interested in the problem of color to look for harmonies special to each painting, and that sometimes a quite lively color scheme betokened a personal observation of nature as well as a keen feeling for the juxtaposition of colors, without regard for the traditional principles of the classical land-scape. This can be seen in *The Thames near Walton Bridge*, painted around 1807. Most of the time, however, in his ambition to equal Claude Lorrain, Turner saw the color of his mythological compositions through the French painter's eyes, and his palette then remained subject to a conventional range of colors. *The Decline of the Carthaginian Empire* of 1817 is an example of this impersonal vision.

If we contrast Turner's second and last period with his first, as is habitually done,

Bonneville, Savoy, 1810   Drawing, 7⁵/₈″ × 11⁵/₁₆″   British Museum, London

it can be noted that he did not become more «colorist.» An almost monochrome tonality, of a golden hue, dominates each painting of this period, and it does not seem to be a particularly realistic expression of the color. This is particularly true of his seascapes, which represent Turner at his peak.

The «colour beginnings» therefore refer to another aspect of his painting. There is first of all a new relationship between color and drawing. Until now Turner had always been attentive to the architecture of a picture and to the carefully studied construction of the various elements that entered into his composition on different levels, and all of these elements were drawn with precision and meticulousness. His fondness for architectural structures, even as a young boy, is well known. Perhaps he also wanted to prove to his colleagues at the Royal Academy how competent he was to be teacher

HONFLEUR, 1830
Watercolor, 5½″ ×7½″   British Museum, London

Basle, 1806—1810   Print of etching worked over in sepia for mezzotinter   From « Liber Studiorum »

of perspective there (he gave up this position in 1837). In all the paintings done in his first period color was visibly secondary to drawing. Without color the picture undoubtedly would not have attained its poetic density. But the drawing, alone, contained the basic subject of the painting. This situation, however, changes completely with the « colour beginnings. »

Turner began to free himself from draughtsmanship through his watercolors. He freed himself in the way in which Monet, some forty years later, was to conceive painting only in terms of his most fleeting visual impressions. Here Turner was the obvious precursor of Impressionism. For him, « colour beginnings » means that he was now beginning to look only at the colors of objects. There is no trace of drawing in these watercolors, which he carefully refrained from exhibiting, as if the time had not yet come to *confess* his discovery of an impalpable world that was nothing but shapes colored

Water - Black Dogs, c. 1812   Drawing, 11⁷/₁₆″ × 18¹/₂″   From « Large Farnley »

with light, and in most cases very pale, masses. It is a strange palette, with milky shades that are barely rose, barely blue, barely yellow. The vague evocations of lakes, bays, rivers, shorelines, and castles in these mysterious landscapes appear through a dazed revery in which each object is transformed into a luminous vapor, an imponderable transparency, as if ready to fade and disappear. The author of the inventory, in a quandary, sometimes attempts to identify a subject *(Windsor Castle?)*, but his question mark reveals his uncertainty.

In some works the delicate *tachisme* of the watercolor is pushed so far in the direction of an abstraction that the subject cannot be defined. In such cases we cannot say whether it is a castle on a hill, or a river with trees under the setting sun. No painter before Turner had given color such resolute autonomy.

The series of small watercolors done at Petworth on bluetinted paper dates

Dogs - Guns - Game - Ale - Barrel, c. 1812   Drawing, $11^7/_{16}$" × $18^1/_2$"   From « Large Farnley »

probably from the beginning of this period. This was not a very successful attempt, because the tint of the paper did not favor the subtle harmonies sought by Turner, who for a large part had to turn to the greater opacities of gouache. But his work has a freedom of stroke that reveals the mastery with which he had accomplished his break from the (often excessively) careful technique of his previous works. He now peopled his pictures with more human beings, since he no longer had to draw them.

Turner was henceforth to remain faithful to this style, which was to make him the most daring and the greatest watercolorist of the nineteenth century, until his last works. Among the works in the R. W. Lloyd bequest, which entered the British Museum after the Turner bequest, we find a few watercolors from the period 1840–1843 — *Lake Nemi, Lucerne by Moonlight* — in which the artist seems to have returned, undoubtedly only temporarily, to his earlier conceptions. Draughtsmanship regains its role, and the exces-

71

sively «worked» color deprives them of that strange lightness so striking in his last period. But because of lack of precision in the dating, it is difficult to say whether we should see in this a weakening of quality, linked to a change of technique with a view to a final style, or whether these watercolors should be regarded as a few isolated cases.

As for the paintings, their appearance too changes, but in a different way. A last echo of Romanticism, resulting however from a sensitive observation of nature and liberated from all narrative concern, appears in two paintings dating from 1828/29: *Arricia: Sunset* and *Archway with Trees by the Sea.* I do not know whether these are the landscapes to which Ruskin alluded in his lecture of November 15, 1853, on «Turner and His Work,» in which he says that «Before Turner, no one had lifted the veil that concealed nature from us,» and «Turner is the first artist to give us a perfect kind of landscape.» In any case, if we may speak of *perfection* in painting, it is certain that such landscapes raise our pleasure of contemplation to its highest degree, and a perfect harmony is thereby established between the painter's vision and its viewer.

But even after these canvases, Turner's discovery of his profound originality still lay ahead of him.

A LIBERATING VISION

The great revolution took place after 1830. It is even possible to pinpoint its occurrence in the paintings commissioned by Lord Egremont and executed by Turner between 1830 and 1837. Perhaps he felt particularly at ease at Petworth House, and more free to express himself far from the Academy. In the house there reigned a friendly, very unconventional atmosphere described by C. F. Greville in his *Journal,* published in 1898, in which he speaks of Egremont as a «discerning, eccentric, and charitable man» at whose home artists were always welcome. He tells us that «Lord Egremont detests etiquette and cannot bear to have anything to do with it; he likes people to come and go as they wish.»

Music Party, The Letter, Figures in Disguise, and especially *Interior at Petworth* are paintings in which, for the first time in the history of painting, color forms indeterminate shapes. These canvases have sometimes been regarded as unfinished works. But no completion is possible. They are no more unfinished than most of the watercolors subsequently painted by Turner, in which a few masses and areas of color suffice to form a landscape.

The single painting by Turner in the Louvre, the *Landscape* of 1835/40 admired by Edmond de Goncourt in the Camille Groult Collection (if it is, however, the same work, which has not been absolutely proven) is even today regarded as another unfinished

Norham Castle, Sunrise, c. 1835–1840
Oil, 35¾″ × 48″   Tate Gallery, London

A Vaulted Hall, c. 1835–1840
Oil, 29½″ × 36″   Tate Gallery, London

STORMY SEA, 1835–1840
Oil, 35¾″ × 48″ Tate Gallery, London

The Deluge, c. 1810   Drawing from «Liber Studiorum»

work. Its subject can barely be ascertained: a hint of a tree, a suspicion of a stream winding toward an intangible stretch of water. It can nevertheless be compared with *The Junction of Severn and Wye,* an engraving from the *Liber Studiorum.* This painting is of major importance for a knowledge of the painter's most beautiful period, and the Louvre is very fortunate to have been able to acquire it in 1967.

   Although they are representative of the last stage of Turner's development and his achievement of a liberating vision of light dissolving forms and colors, these paintings did not prevent him (especially when he wanted to exhibit at the Royal Academy) from sometimes expressing himself with greater precision and endowing certain compositions with a more studied structure, at least in some portion of the painting, in which case a boat, a fragment of a building, or a figure then becomes the only symbol of a tangible reality. The manner in which Turner lays his colors on the canvas seems to correspond

VENICE: THE GRAND CANAL (ABOVE THE RIALTO), 1839
Watercolor, $7\,{}^{3}/_{5}''\times 11\,{}^{1}/_{5}''$ British Museum, London

VENICE: PUNTA DELLA SALUTE, 1819
Watercolor, 9″ × 11 ³/₅″   British Museum, London

to this differentiation of areas of interest. A few details alone on the almost completely smooth surface are treated with a slight impasto that catches the light.

The sky and the sea, which Turner had always loved to paint, also changed. Whereas formely he had sought to depict in striking fashion the «sculptural» side of the water, those violent movements and reliefs of the waves that so often charmed him (as in 1803 in *The Calais Pier,* and in 1817 in *The Entrance to the Meuse*), henceforth he devoted himself to conveying atmospheric impressions, and they alone are the real subject. Despite its title, *Staffa, Fingal's Cave,* exhibited in 1832 at the Royal Academy (now in the collection of Lord Astor of Hever), leaves the rocky coast of Staffa Island practically invisible under the strange glimmerings spread over the vast stretch of the sky by a faintly pink setting sun. The center of interest of the painting is the uncoiling of the dark smoke coming from the boat, whose outline remains hazy in a dark area of the sea.

On October 16, 1834, Turner watched the burning of the Houses of Parliament in London. He made several watercolors of the scene, which differ considerably from the two oil versions (one in the Philadelphia Museum, the other in the Cleveland Museum) painted during the following year. In these paintings, and very visibly in the latter, the painter has not tried in any way to make «picturesque» use of the event. He makes us participants in a great revery before this spectable which is transforming the evening into a kind of aurora borealis, with the fiery sky reflected in the Thames.

At Venice (in 1835?) Turner painted numerous watercolors in which he applied his new conception of color. For several years he made use of them in composing evocations of this city, which he visited for the last time in 1840, and where each of his visits was a stage on the road of his liberation from pictorial conventions. Although these watercolors are executed directly with the brush, without any drawing for support (I examined them with a magnifying glass and saw no trace of pencil), he filled his sketchbooks with countless drawings. Quick sketches, their light but precise lines drawn with black lead, and sometimes supplemented with color notes, are juxtaposed in disorder on the sheets (I counted as many as eighteen sketches on a single page), with the Palace of the Doges and La Salute, the rigging of a sailing vessel and the pillars of a church standing side by side, as if the painter wanted to economize on paper — which is very possible.

Turner kept his most trifling sketches. In the boxes in which they are stored in the British Museum, we saw hundreds of minuscule, sometimes tattered bits of paper on which he had captured some impression in a few lines. He drew on the margins of his maps, and a few outlines of ships illustrate the back of one of his visiting cards, which reads:

Mr. J. M. W. Turner
47 Queen Ann Street, Harley Street.

Other drawings, on single sheets of white or gray tinted paper, have been gone over with ink or chalk. Their dating is uncertain. Among the views of cities, rivers, mountains, and castles are a few pencil and red crayon female nudes, sometimes touched up with pink or white gouache, drawn with diligence and sensuality. They are rare in Turner's work, and we know to what aberration we owe the disappearance of the painter's

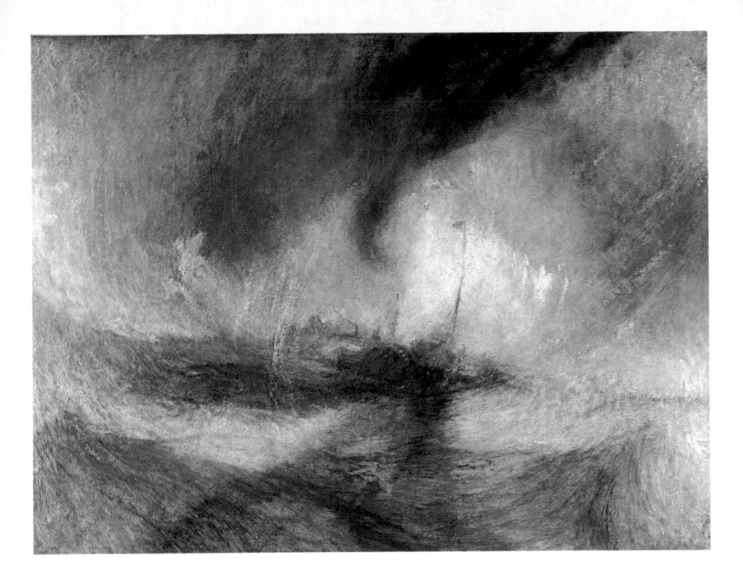

Snow Storm: Steam-Boat off a Harbour's Mouth..., 1842
Oil, 36″ × 48″ Tate Gallery, London

VENICE, c. 1840
Oil, 24″ × 36″   Victoria and Albert Museum, London

LA DOGANA AND SANTA MARIA DELLA SALUTE, VENICE, c. 1843
Oil. 24⅜″ × 36⅝″   National Gallery of Art, Washington D.C. (Gift of the Fuller Foundation)

RAIN, STEAM AND SPEED: THE GREAT WESTERN RAILWAY, c. 1840 Oil, 35″ × 48″ Tate Gallery, London

erotic drawings. In his book *My Life and Loves,* Frank Harris devoted a chapter to John Ruskin, in which he relates the latter's remarks on this subject. Here are the essential passages:

When upon his death Turner bequeathed his paintings to the nation, I went to see them. I found them still in their boxes in the sub-basements of the National Gallery; no one was taking care of them, and no one seemed to appreciate their value. I wrote concerning this matter to the Prime Minister, who if I remember correctly was Lord Palmerston, telling him that I should be particularly proud to be authorized to file and catalogue Turner's work. He put me in touch with the museum's administrators, and I was duly entrusted with this task. Throughout 1857 and half of the following year, I continued my work. . . . One day, upon opening a carton, I found it full of drawings and paintings of the most shameful sort, depicting women's sexual organs, drawings that to me were completely inexcusable and inexplicable. I decided to find out whence came these ignominies, and discovered that every Friday my hero left his house in Chelsea and went to Wapping, where he stayed until Monday morning, living with the sailors' girls and painting them in every posture of lewdness. . . . What should I do? For weeks I was tormented with doubts, trying to raise my mind to the highest moral level. Finally, like a bolt out of the blue, the idea came to me that I had been selected as the only man capable of making a major decision in the matter. I immediately burned those hundreds of lewd sketches and paintings. . . . Yes, I burned them all! Do you not think I was right? I'm proud, very proud, to have done it.

Needless to say, far from feeling he was right, Frank Harris was angered by Ruskin's assumption of the right to destroy those works. It was an action for which he cannot be pardoned.

Many facts in Turner's existence have remained hidden. At this time he was living with a Mrs. Booth, with whom he had probably become acquainted early in the 1830s, and who had become his housekeeper. He had purchased her house, saying, «I shall live here, and people will call me Mr. Booth.» He spent the last years of his life with her, and gave her back her house when he died.

SOLITUDE AND GLORY

Between 1841 and 1844 Turner made several trips to Switzerland. His sketchbooks reveal that the principal places visited were Bern, Lucerne, Interlaken, the Lake of Zug, Basel, Lausanne, and also the banks of the Rhine. However, his most important paintings during this period relate to England.

Turin Cathedral (Façade of San Giovanni), 1819
Pencil, 4⅜" × 7⅜" British Museum, London

In *Peace — Burial at Sea,* an octagonal painting dating from 1842, he repeats, in a different manner and with a more powerful contrast between shadow and light, the effect of smoke trailing across the sky that he had used ten years earlier in *Staffa, Fingal's Cave.* Here the greater importance given to the ship is justified by the subject of the painting — the funeral at sea of Sir David Wilkie — but the details of the vessel are not made any more visible for that reason, and in this characteristic Turner's vision can be said to be truly « impressionist.» In this connection, let us relate, as Marcel Proust did in his preface to his translation of Ruskin's *The Bible of Amiens*, the following anecdote relative to Turner:

One day he was drawing the port of Plymouth and a few vessels, a mile or two offshore, seen against the light. Having shown this drawing to a naval officer, the latter remarked with surprise, and objected with a very understandable indignation, that the ships of the line had no portholes. « No.» said Turner, « Of course not. If you climb Mount Edgecumbe and look at the vessels against the light, you'll see that you cannot perceive the portholes.» « Very well,» said the officer, still indignant, « but you know that there are portholes there?» « Yes,» Turner answered, « of course I know that, but my job is to draw what I see, not what I know.»

However, Turner also knew how to paint what he did not see, or at least what he saw only in his imagination. And his imagination carried him closer and closer to an intellectual conception of painting in which poetry and metaphysics were able to meet. For it must not be thought that this son of a barber had remained uneducated. On the contrary, those close to him were impressed by his literary knowledge. He had acquired it alone, with the same ambition and determination that he had applied to becoming a great painter. He did a great deal of reading in the poets and philosophers, and had himself written a long poem, « The Fallacies of Hope,» in which his lofty spiritual interests are reflected.

As he aged, a sometimes dramatic vision asserted itself in his paintings. (His work, moreover, is full of scenes of catastrophes.) When in 1843 he painted that strange square canvas entitled *Light and Color (Goethe's Theory) — The Day after the Flood*, as a counterpoint to another painting, *Shadow and Darkness — The Evening of the Flood*, he enclosed his subject in a globe of light, which gives the composition both its rotating movement and its cosmic significance. This homage to Goethe, no doubt sincere, was also a statement about his own color preferences, because the translation of Goethe's theory was not published in England until 1840, and long before then Turner had favored yellow in the color scheme of his paintings, particularly in his seascapes and in certain landscapes which were estranged from naturalism by such coloring. In 1827 one critic, shocked to see that everything produced by Turner's brush was, as he put it, « afflicted with jaundice,» had reproached him for this preference.

But paintings in which Turner tried to apply an ideological system based on a symbolism of structure and color are rather rare. From this time on, his romantic imagination, or rather the avatars of this imagination, adapted to his new pictorial conception, led him to transcend nature, or any scene observed in the external world, and to impart to it an unwonted resonance which sometimes acquires the character of a grandiose, fantastic dream.

Here Turner's genius was expressed with a wonderful freedom that was, however, severely judged by his contemporaries. The masterpiece of this period is *Rain, Steam, and Speed — The Great Western Railway* of 1844, a view from the recently constructed bridge between Maidenhead and Teplow, linking the valley of the Thames with Devonshire. The Great Western was at that time the fastest railroad in Europe; it traveled at a speed of more than 90 mph, which seemed to be a terrifying accomplishment. People spoke of it as they would of an apocalyptic machine, just as the French had talked some years earlier of the modest «Paris-Saint-Germain» (which did not exceed 25 mph), referred to by Théophile Gautier as «a rather stupid invention.»

This prophetic image of a future world, the world of machines, is integrated harmoniously into Turner's musing vision of a landscape under rain. The smoke escaping from the locomotive is the gentle bond linking it with the sky. The idea of speed is technically depicted by the haziness of the railroad cars, in accordance with a method reminiscent of the manner used by Giacomo Balla in 1912 to depict movement in his Futurist paintings (*Dynamism of a Dog on a Leash, Girl and Balcony*). But Turner, discreetly and almost ironically, also imparts to the idea of speed its dimension of relativity by making a hare run along the track.

When we turn to the paintings of his first period, in which not only his penchant for architectural structures but also his attention to the structure and drawing of the painting and the rational, classical organization of the spaces are so apparent, we could almost believe that the artist who cares little for these concerns and sees the world only through an approximate vision of forms is a different painter. All realist precision has disappeared, and the color itself seems to spring from a phantasm of the imagination in which every object, infused with a light whose source cannot always be divined, carries us to the threshold of an unreal universe. Here Turner stands in opposition to both the esthetics of all the painters of his age and his own earlier conceptions which he had long been applying. From this time on his work seems, irreversibly, to be in revolt against these very conceptions.

In this last phase of his development we can see the close relationship, through their expressive quality and their technique, between the canvases which remain linked to a material fact, like the painting of the passing of the Great Western Railway, and those inspired by apocalyptic subjects, like *The Angel Standing in the Sun* of 1846.

At the age of seventy, Turner was continuing his search for landscapes in the English countryside and on the Continent. We can follow his itinerary in Switzerland in 1844, and in 1845 we find him on the French coast, at Boulogne, Dieppe, Le Tréport, and Eu, where King Louis-Philippe had him to dinner. However, his health was declining, and now he rarely sent a painting to the Royal Academy. One of his last pictures, painted in 1850, takes up an episode from the story of Dido, and seems to proclaim his approaching end. It is entitled *The Visit to the Tomb*.

He lived in great solitude in his house at Cheyne Walk, Chelsea, near his beloved Thames. Here he died peacefully on December 19, 1851, his face caressed by a ray of sun which entered through the window and came to rest on his bed. He was buried in St. Paul's Cathedral, where, as he had desired, he rests in the crypt between the tombs of Joshua Reynolds and Thomas Lawrence, not far from the coffin of Nelson, whose death he had depicted in his painting *The Battle of Trafalgar*.

During his lifetime Turner's success with the critics fluctuated constantly. He was never worried about being misunderstood, and while he had his detractors, he also had many admirers and purchasers. Nevertheless, at his death his studio still contained more than three hundred canvases and approximately two thousand watercolors and

BELLINZONA, 1844
Watercolor, 9$^1/_5$″ × 13$^1/_5$″   British Museum, London

90

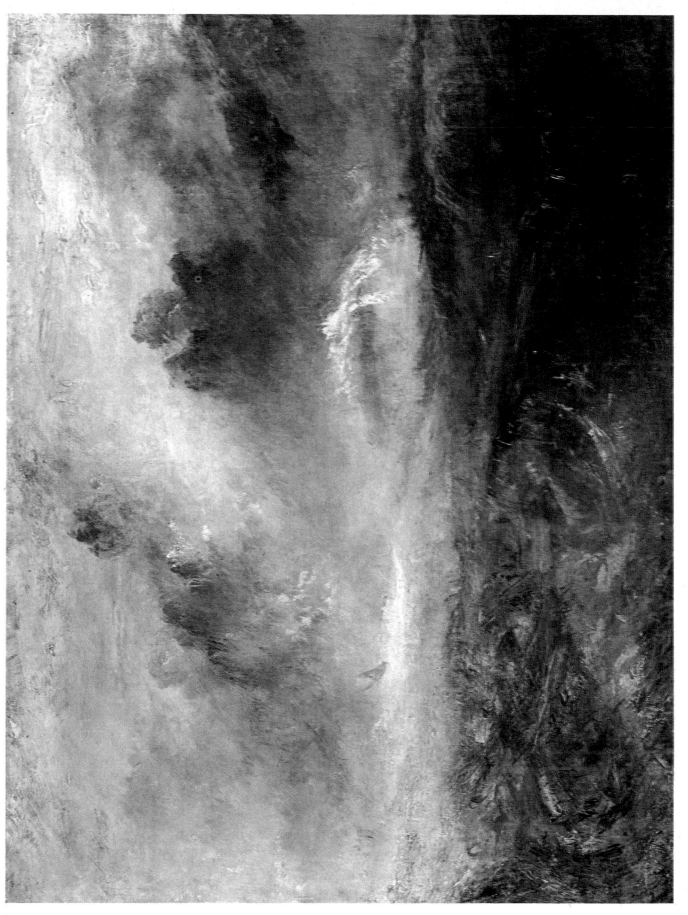

Rough Sea with Wreckage, c. 1834–1840   Oil, 36¼″ × 48¼″   Tate Gallery, London

drawings, which he bequeathed to the State and which are preserved today in London's museums, chiefly the Tate Gallery and the British Museum. He also left the sum of 60,000 pounds for the establishment of an institution for unfortunate or sick artists.

Turner's importance was only very gradually recognized in England, and more gradually still outside his own country. The very persons who had been most strongly influenced by him never openly acknowledged what they owed to his art. Undoubtedly we cannot know exactly which of his canvases Monet and Pissarro saw in London in 1870, and it is almost certain that they did not see his watercolors, but Monet's subsequent criticisms concerning Turner prove how much attention the French artist had paid to his painting.

Turner had never bothered to exhibit his canvases in France, where during his lifetime only a few of his engravings, at most, were known. He had visited Delacroix in Paris — probably in 1833 — and the Frenchman had admired his style of painting, despite his uncomplimentary report of the visit in his Journal: « He made an indifferent impression on me; he looked like an English farmer, with his black, rather vulgar clothes, heavy shoes, and hard, cold expression » (March 24, 1855). J. K. Huysmans spoke competently of his « volatilized landscapes. » Gustave Planche was one of his defenders, while finding flaws which he attributed to « the depravation of a singularly strong nature. » Neither Elie Faure nor Venturi understood him. In one of his stylistic flights the former said, oddly enough, that « He rose so high that the excessively rarefied air could not support his flight, » and « Turner conceals the poverty of his color under fire-works. » Venturi judged Turner to be « very inferior » to Constable and Bonington, whom in truth he left far beneath him.

As for Ruskin, who was a friend of the painter during his last ten years, and who was the first to analyze his work sympathetically and with a sincere effort at comprehension, he nevertheless appears to have sometimes failed to view Turner's painting correctly. When he wrote, « Of all people, he is the only one who ever gave nature her own colors, » he did not perceive that in the landscapes in which Turner gave striking proof of his genius, nature was clothed in purely imaginary colors. But perhaps he was right when he said upon his death that, « It is through these eyes, closed forever at the bottom of the tomb, that generations as yet unborn will see nature. »

BIOGRAPHY

1775 Birth of Joseph Mallord William Turner, eldest son of William Turner, barber and hairdresser, on April 23, at 21 Maiden Lane, Covent Garden, London.

1789 First known sketch book, the *Oxford Sketch Book*. Works with the painter Thomas Melton. Accepted as a student at the Royal Academy School.

1790 Exhibits for the first time (a watercolor) at the Royal Academy.

1792 Travels around Wales, the first of many travels throughout England. Numerous drawings of the countryside.

1793 Receives a prize from the Society of Arts for a landscape drawing. Visits Rochester, Canterbury, Dover, and other cities.

1794 First engraving made from one of his watercolors. Probably begins to attend the watercolor courses at Dr. Monro's school, in the company of Thomas Girtin. Works there for three years.

1795 Visits southern Wales, Sussex, and the Ile of Wight.

1796 Exhibits an oil painting for the first time at the Royal Academy: *Fishermen at Sea*. Exhibits there annually thereafter.

1799 Elected an Associate Member of the Royal Academy. Takes up residence at 64 Harley Street with the actress Sarah Danby.

1801 First trip to Scotland.

1802 Elected full Member of the Royal Academy. First trip to France; stays for a time in Paris.

1804 Death of his mother in an insane asylum.

1805 Exhibits his works in the gallery he has opened in his home on Harley Street.

1807 Publication of the first series of engravings of the *Liber Studiorum*. Appointed professor of perspective at the Royal Academy.

1808 First visit to Sir John Leicester, at Tabley House in Cheshire.

1809 First visit to Lord Egremont, at Petworth in Sussex.

1810 Fist visit to Walter Fawkes, at Farnley Hall in Yorkshire. Moves from Harley Street to 47 Queen Ann Street.

1811 Travels in Dorset, Devon, Cornwall, and Somerset.

1816 Visits the north of England.

1817 Tours Belgium ((Waterloo), Holland, and the banks of the Rhine.

1818 Visits Edinburgh.

1819 First tour of Italy: Turin, Lake Como, Venice, Rome, Naples, Florence. Returns via Mont Cenis.

1821 New private gallery in his home in Queen Ann Street. Trip to France.

1822 Spends some time in Scotland during George IV's visit.

1823 Visits southeast coast of England. Receives commission for a painting, *The Battle of Trafalgar,* for St. James's Palace.

1825 Holland, Belgium, banks of the Rhine.

1826 Meuse and Moselle rivers, Brittany, valley of the Loire.

1828 Another trip to France; second tour of Italy.

1829 Paris, Normandy, Brittany, Touraine, etc. On September 21, death of his father.

1830 In the Midlands. His new style begins to develop.

1831 Scotland.

1832 Illustrations for Walter Scott.

1833 In Paris. Probably visited Delacroix and made another trip to Italy (or in 1835?).

1834 Meuse, Moselle, and Rhine rivers. Watches the burning of the Houses of Parliament in London.

1836 France, Switzerland, Val d'Aosta.

1840 Meets John Ruskin. Another trip to Venice.

1841 Switzerland.

1842 Switzerland.

1844 Switzerland and the Rhine.

1845 Boulogne, Dieppe, Le Tréport. Invited to dinner, at Eu, by King Louis-Philippe.

1851 Turner dies in London on December 19, at his home at 119 Cheyne Walk, Chelsea. Is buried in St. Paul's Cathedral on December 30.

BIBLIOGRAPHY

1834   L. Ritchie. *Turner's Annual Tours.*

1862   Walter Thornbury. *The Life of J. M. W. Turner, R. A.,* 2 vol.

1902   Sir Walter Armstrong. *Turner.*

1909   A. J. Finberg. *Complete Inventory of the Drawings of the Turner Bequest,* 2 vols.

1924   A. J. Finberg. *The History of Turner's* Liber Studiorum with a new Catalogue raisonné.

1925   T. Ashby. *Turner's Visions of Rome.*

1930   A. J. Finberg. *In Venice with Turner.*

1939   A. J. Finberg. *The Life of J. M. W. Turner, R. A.*
Camille Mauclair. *Turner.* IIyperion.

1949   Douglas Cooper. *Turner.*

1962   Martin Butlin. *Turner Watercolours.*

1964   Michael Kitson. *Turner.*

1965   Mary Chamot. *Turner Early Works.*
Martin Butlin. *Turner Later Works.*

1966   Lawrence Gowing. *Turner: Imagination and Reality.*
Jack Lindsay. *J. M. W. Turner, His Life and Work.*

1969   John Gage. *Colour in Turner, Poetry and Truth.*
Graham Reynolds. *Turner.*

1971   William Gaunt. *Turner.*

1972   Gerald Wilkinson. *Turner's early Sketchbooks.*
John Gage. *Turner. Rain, Steam and Speed.*

1974   Gerald Wilkinson. *The Sketches of Turner, R. A., 1802–1820.*

ILLUSTRATIONS